# JACKIE

# Jackie

## A Caregiver's Story

Ronald Lombard

Copyright © 2008 by Ronald Lombard.

| | | |
|---|---|---|
| Library of Congress Control Number: | | 2008906552 |
| ISBN: | Hardcover | 978-1-4363-5799-9 |
| | Softcover | 978-1-4363-5798-2 |

All rights reserved. No part of this book may be reproduced or transmitted in any form or by any means, electronic or mechanical, including photocopying, recording, or by any information storage and retrieval system, without permission in writing from the copyright owner.

This book was printed in the United States of America.

**To order additional copies of this book, contact:**
Xlibris Corporation
1-888-795-4274
www.Xlibris.com
Orders@Xlibris.com
51504

# Contents

Biography ........................................................................... 7

Letters of Excerpt ............................................................. 9

Prologue ........................................................................... 11

A Caregiver's Story: Overview; Summary of Events ........ 17

Part One:    A Caregiver's Story ....................................... 21

Part One:    A Caregiver's Story: Final Comments ......... 43

Part Two:    A Caregiver's Story: the Final Journey ....... 45

Part Three:  A Caregiver's Story: Grievance .................... 63

Part Four:   A Caregiver's Story, Closing Remarks .......... 87

Acknowledgments ............................................................ 89

# Biography

What a beautiful life Jackie and I had together in which she gave me three now-grown children: Wendy, Ron Jr., and Suzanne. My oldest daughter is a graduate of Tufts University and the University of Michigan School of Public Health, and is now working as a program evaluator of kidney disease prevention programs. My youngest daughter attended Becker Jr. College and is a certified nurse assistant in private care. My son is a graduate of Lowell University and owns his own consulting business with over two hundred employees. I also have eight beautiful grandchildren—I have been truly blessed.

I have an associate of science degree in food management from the University of Massachusetts and have worked both blue-collar and professionally, but nothing has ever so affected my life as when Jackie asked me to be her caregiver, the hardest job I have ever had. However, it would turn out to be the most rewarding. Not a writer by trade, it was difficult for me personally to put this story together; but the nature of my wife's disease, her courage, and her devotion to me and to our family gave me inspiration to honor her with a legacy she so deserved. She was elated that someone else might benefit by telling her story. I also received much inspiration from all the health workers who touched our lives, such as doctors, nurses, and home health aids.

And I am particularly thankful to my children and neighbors for their loving support all through Jackie's illness.

No research was done to write this story; it was written from my heart and from my soul and inspired to completion by my wife's spirit and the guardian angels of the hospice team from the University of Massachusetts Medical Center.

# Letters of Excerpt

Medical Group
Family Medicine

24 Julio Drive
Shrewsbury, MA 01545
Tel: 508-845-1436
Fax: 508-842-3005
www.umassmemorial.org

Joseph F. Daigneault, MD
Ingrid Fuller, MD
Michael A. Burdulis, MD
Roxanne Latimer, MD

Olivo Ponto Cerebellar Atrophy, or O.P.C.A. for short, is a brain disorder which invariably fills its victim and family with the deepest dread. O.P.C.A. is actually a rare group of brain diseases that involves the brain stem and cerebellum. The unfortunate patient can expect a stepwise decline in bodily functions ultimately leading to death.

The initial clumsiness and unsteady gait is, with time, accompanied by slurring of the speech, difficulty swallowing and rigidity of the limbs. A spectrum of other symptoms can variably afflict the victim depending on the subtype of O.P.C.A. Symptoms include constipation, difficulty urinating, tremors, vision impairment, muscle spasms, drooling and loss of ability to speak.

Despite the dramatic symptoms, it is still not clear why the brain undergoes this severe degeneration, although several gene anomalies are now being linked to some subtypes of the disease.

The physician cannot offer his or her struggling patient any hope of a cure. Stalling the inexorable downward spiral of health and loss of independence is extremely difficult to do, with the limitations of currently available medications. Mostly these efforts are unsuccessful.

Much of the medical care in O.P.C.A. involves management of the symptoms, supporting the patient as he or she struggles to survive. This disease is not infectious, yet its negative effects will spread with time, to put an enormous strain on the patient's caregiver. Olivo Ponto Cerebellar Atrophy's effects also ripple out to the surrounding community as, to name but a few, extended family, hospice workers, clergy, equipment purveyors, and even carpenters are involved in the care process.

Jackie Lombard struggled with this disease for years before it prematurely took her life. Early in the disease process Jackie surprised me with a little rug that she had hooked by hand. I love its brilliant smiley face design. Jackie and her loving husband Ron fought O.P.C.A. with a positive spirit and my monthly visits were often accompanied by much laughter.

Ron's story is an extraordinary tale of unwavering dedication and strength, a love story where a glimmering smile breaks through the darkness of despair.

Ingrid Fuller MD

*UMass Memorial Medical Group is a multi-specialty group practice with offices throughout Central Massachusetts.*

My beloved mother-in-law Jackie and I shared many things in common. We loved to garden, laugh, read and we had a passion for good food and good wine. Most of all, however, we shared a love for her son, Lee. It was this love that ultimately bonded us together. Jackie was much more than my mother-in –law, she was my friend.

Over the years we shared many celebrations together and it was fun to watch our family grow and I loved to see Jackie with our children as she adored them all so very much. Jackie loved to hold them on her lap and read to them as babies. Her illness took hold when my youngest child, Stephanie, was only one. Her illness did not, however, keep her from seeing and loving her grandchildren. Lee and I would bring them all to see her on Sundays and they would love to crawl in bed with her and watch TV and play with all her "devices". Jackie's face would light up and beam whenever my husband, Lee, walked in the room; it was evident to see how deep her love was for her family and even without the use of her voice, her eyes spoke volumes.

I loved my mother-in-law deeply and was very saddened when her disease progressed to impair and ultimately deplete her speech and mobility. It never depleted her smile or the sparkle in her eyes and I will always remember her with great love and affection. Lee and I enjoy reliving her more vibrant years with our children. We love to share stories and photos of Jackie, along with funny family "episodes" from years gone by. Jackie is alive and well in our memories and in the smiles and expressions of our three children, Matthew, Michael and Stephanie.

My life is better for having known Jackie as she is ultimately the reason I have such a beautiful family. I will always be grateful to her for that.

Angela Lombard

# Prologue

The first part of this story was printed in the National Ataxia Foundation's quarterly magazine called *Generations,* which appeared in their April 2006 issue. I received so much positive input from doctors, nurses, home health aids, caregivers, and nursing home administrators and family that it encouraged me to write the middle and end results of being a caregiver. It is my hope that this book will help promote stem cell research and give hope to the many caregivers across the country that have one of the hardest jobs imaginable, trying to cope with brain ataxia.

Dying is not an easy process no matter what the illness is because most people who have a loved one with a terminal illness only see them for a few hours per day and don't see the struggle that goes on from morning until night. But multiple-system degeneration robs the patient of everything. And if you don't think it can happen to you, then it suffices me to say, "Don't count on it." Look at Ronald Reagan as a good example when it was discovered that he had Alzheimer's disease and most recently Charlton Hesston, who kept himself in good physical condition both mentally and physically.

Alzheimer's is the beginning of dementia and can strike the strongest people of all ages and gender. People suffering from ataxia can have Parkinson's, multiple sclerosis, Lou Gehrig's, and a whole host of diseases that affect the brain. So it behooves the population to promote stem cell research even more than what is presently under way as countless men and women could be saved from early demise caused by protein and gene malfunction. For our nation has endured a Congress that has done little when it comes to health care and money needed for research. We all should have at least as good health care coverage as enjoyed by most government employees. The failure of the U.S. government to put money into health care is shameful, dishonest, greedy, and disingenuous of our elected officials. They have failed because politicians don't listen to the people anymore except to answer to big business.

The United States used to have the best health care in the world. Now we have become so selfish in pursuit of the all-mighty dollar that we have left forty-seven million people without health insurance while members of Congress enjoy the very best health care for themselves.

Because our country has for-profit health care, the best care goes to those who can afford it. Those who can't afford it get the worst care or none at all. Insurance companies are notorious for withholding coverage for patients in order to boost profits.

According to *Wikipedia*, we are the only industrialized, wealthy nation that does not have a universal health care system. We spend more money than any other country on health care, yet we still have forty-seven million uninsured people and many more whose health insurance is inadequate to cover the high costs of medical care. The inability to pay one's medical bills has become the leading reason for personal bankruptcy. So we are now thirty-seventh place in the world in overall performance. To me that is shocking.

## Jackie

President Bush is giving our taxpayers' money to Iraq to pay for infrastructure, and all this while Iraq has some thirty to sixty billion dollars sitting in American banks and is paying nothing to support their own needs. Instead of charity for foreign nations, we should be using these funds for health care and other critical needs in our own country.

It is through this book that I give thanks to all the doctors, nurses, home health aides, speech therapists, music therapist, religious counselors, grief counselors, massage therapists, and all the other caring professionals who work for or align themselves with the hospice program at the University of Massachusetts Medical Center in Worcester, Massachusetts. Jackie and I were blessed to be part of this hospice team during the last year of her life, for no greater gift can you give a loved one with a terminal illness than to keep them at home. When you have experienced a long and difficult illness, it doesn't take long to see the bigger picture in which all of us are uniquely here to help each other and may even be preordained by God's will without ever knowing it. If only 1 percent of the universe was like Earth, there would be a billion habitable planets. So I don't think we are alone in this world, and if one were to compare Earth with the universe, it would be no bigger than a grain of sand on the beach. This journey that we are all in will return us all like a glass of ocean water back to the sea.

Ron and Jackie (1958, Senior Reception)

Jackie and Oldest Daughter Wendy at
National Seashore, Cape Cod, Massachusetts

# A Caregiver's Story

## Summary of Needed Adaptations

*First-Year Retrograde*

- Walking when holding on to grab bars or using a walker
- Safety bars needed in bathroom, particularly around the toilet
- A railing had to be built across the stairway in hallway
- All scatter rugs or runners taken up
- A portable wheelchair by Invacare; it was light, maneuverable, and great for traveling.

*Second-Year Retrograde*

- The purchase of an electric wheelchair—Jazzy 1113; it was small and went through doorways easy. Patient was able to use it for shopping, doctor's visits, or social occasions
- Need for a wheelchair ramp
- Started spending more time in bed
- Unable to use electric toothbrush alone
- Eyesight diminished
- More rigidity

- Catheterization increased to three per day. Patient has always only been able to void about 20 percent. We were constantly transferring patient to toilet or commode because the bladder was always full. Ditropan caused too many side effects, so we stopped using it. Tremors became worse, and the doctor ordered tizanidine muscle relaxant.
- Speech becoming slurred

### *Third- and Fourth-Year Retrograde*

- Speech retrograding with no stopping point
- Legs stiff as boards
- Dexterity lost
- Sleep disorders
- Headaches
- Dysphagia

### *Fifth-Year Retrograde*

- Almost total loss of speech
- Total loss of right leg movement; right arm only 5 percent use
- Difficulty moving bowels
- Became totally bedridden

### *Sixth-Year Retrograde*

- Hospice needed
- Eye movement and some ability to use finger pressure
- Chest crackle; use hyoscyamine (Levsin) to help breathing

- Oxygen twenty-four hours a day as needed
- Scopolamine patches to help breathing
- Morphine as needed
- Daily massage of neck, face, eyebrows, shoulders, mouth, back, and legs

# Part One: A Caregiver's Story

How do you say no to a woman who had been an outstanding mother and homemaker for the last forty-five years? A beautiful spirit who always put her children's needs before her own? A devoted and compassionate spouse who made the world a better place to live for her whole family? After being diagnosed with a debilitating, degenerative, and ultimately fatal illness, it finally was her turn for somebody else to take care of her.

In May 2000, my wife Jacqueline (Jackie) was diagnosed with a form of multiple system atrophy (MSA) called olivopontocerebellar atrophy (OPCA). This disease affects one out of every one hundred thousand people, so it is quite rare. Hers was labeled "sporadic," meaning not hereditary, although as of yet there is no genetic marker for testing other family members. She was sixty years old at the time, and her diagnosis came after several years of feeling unwell. Her initial symptoms included headaches, dizzy spells, fatigue, nausea, and an overwhelming feeling of malaise, and occasional bruises. Various trips to the doctor had revealed little other than *H. pylori* (the bacteria that can lead to ulcers) and a urinary tract infection (UTI) that had given Jackie no symptoms. These were treated successfully, but UTIs kept recurring. During this time she also started seeing a therapist and taking Paxil since she knew something was wrong, but her doctor could find no physical reason for her health complaints. She felt that it might be depression that was causing her physical symptoms.

On hindsight, there had been some warning signs many years before the ataxia was identified. For example, she might be changing her clothes and I would see a bruise on her hip or elbow. I would ask her, "How did you do that?" and she would answer, "I did it while vacuuming," or "I lost my balance." There were many times when it would take Jackie twice as long as normal to urinate or move her bowels. We assumed that maybe she was just tense at those times. It wasn't until her fifty-ninth birthday that clear signs of something seriously wrong started to appear. These included walking crooked and staggering, especially on inclined surfaces, and bumping the curbs while driving her car.

It was my youngest daughter who pointed out one day that Jackie was walking as though she were very drunk when she only had one glass of wine at dinner meals only. It is easy to see why this disease used to be referred to as drunken sailor syndrome. I used to joke about it with Jackie about her driving until one day she drove right up on a sidewalk. This was the last time I let her drive by herself. (Note: Jackie voluntarily stopped driving not too long after this incident because she realized that she was endangering others as well as herself. However, she was very insulted when the registry of motor vehicles took away her license after doctors notified them about her OPCA.)

Trying to determine the cause of Jackie's worsening symptoms was a long exhausting and sometimes painful process. We made numerous visits to physicians and neurologists, and Jackie endured a battery of x-rays, MRIs, brain scans, physical and psychological testing, and blood work. Jackie had so many needles stuck in her that she often said her body felt like a pincushion. One year later, after seeking another opinion from a third neurologist, who specializes in movement disorders, we finally had a diagnosis. The images taken of Jackie's brain indicated that portions of her brain (olive, pons, cerebellum) were shrinking (atrophying), hence the name olivopontocerebellar atrophy. It was very traumatic for Jackie to have endured so much testing only to find out that there is no cure for OPCA, and there is no definitive treatment for the many different symptoms that occur during the course of the disease. Much of what we have learned has been through trial and error, and approaches in managing symptoms in an ataxia patient need to be tailored to the specific needs of each patient and his or her support network. In the following pages, I will share our experience, and hopes that this information will help others who are coping with this devastating disease.

Jackie's symptoms started out with the inability to completely empty her bladder when urinating, parkinsonian-like trembling of her arms and hands, and 50 percent loss of mobility of the right arm and leg, which retrograded to 80 percent after one year, slurring her words, and impaired eyesight. Balance was bad from day 1, which is why this disease used to be called drunken sailor syndrome before anyone could identify different types of ataxia. She would get occasional headaches, which usually could be eased with acetaminophen or aspirin.

Finding the right medications and supplements to help manage Jackie's symptoms has been an ongoing process of seeing what works best. Building the body's resistance and controlling tremble were goals from the start. The following medications were what my wife was taking as she entered into her seventh year of living with OPCA:

1. Vitamin C (1500 mg per day. We use Ester-C, which is easier on the stomach)
2. Cranberry pills (400 mg caplets, one per day)
3. Cranberry juice and blueberry juice (to stop bacteria build up in the bladder)
4. Clonazepam (0.5 mg; one at bedtime and doubled at end of fifth year)
5. Paroxetine (40 mg daily for depression)
6. Wellbutrin (150 mg once a day for depression)
7. Tizanidine (4 mg-1/2 pill at breakfast and lunch. One full pill at bedtime as muscle relaxant; ranitidine or Zantac [150 mg-one before breakfast and one before dinner])
8. Vitamin E (400 IU)
9. Mucinex (to keep chest congestion loose or as needed [stopped using at fifth-year mark because patient lost the ability to expectorate and could choke on her own mucus])
10. Levaquin (antibiotic; used as needed to control UTI)
11. Ecotrin (81 mg)
12. Fruit-Eze (4 tbsp per day [pureed prunes, dates, raisins, and prune juice])
13. Centrum Silver (one per day)

We did not have any positive results from using coenzyme Q10. Jackie took up to 1,000 mg for up to four months. That doesn't mean you should stop experimenting because some patients say it works for them. We also have not had positive results from some of the Parkinson's medications, such as Mirapex, which made the patient so tired that she couldn't function at all physically. We tried baclofen for spasticity, hoping incontinence would lessen, but it made for frequent accidents.

## Year One

During the year following her diagnosis, Jackie's ability to walk declined dramatically, and she started falling down without any warning. Her neurologist, Dr. Paula Ravin of the University of Massachusetts Memorial Hospital in Worcester, Massachusetts, ordered Jackie a walker. At first, she used one without wheels, but it was too difficult for her to maneuver due to her shaky balance. We replaced it with one that had wheels and brakes that went on when Jackie leaned forward on the handles. This was very effective at helping prevent falls for about the first year.

Other measures to reduce the risk of falling included pulling up all scatter rugs and runners and installing safety (grab) bars throughout the house, especially in the bathroom and most importantly around the toilet and in the shower. Going up and down the stairs became increasingly risky. While our house is a ranch, the laundry area was in the basement, and Jackie insisted she was still able to do the wash. She navigated the stairs using the railing and strategically placed grab bars, but after a while, this became too dangerous. We installed a wooden railing across the top of the basement staircase to prevent Jackie from accidentally falling down the stairs when she went into the back hallway, which she needed to do, to throw away trash and enter/exit the house.

As walking became more and more difficult, we obtained a portable wheelchair by Invacare (DLX model). We liked this one because it was strong and stable, so that Jackie could safely transfer into and out of it. It also was relatively light and maneuverable so she could use it all around the house. It folded to fit in the trunk of our car and made traveling to doctors' appointments and stores much easier for Jackie to endure.

Jackie no longer felt safe in her own home due to her occasional and unpredictable falling episodes. She also was worried about something happening to her when I was outside or away from the house, so we decided to install a Lifeline. While we have only had to use this service once, it was an invaluable asset in those early months for giving Jackie and myself peace of mind when I had to be away from her.

Tremors started to interfere with Jackie's ability to write and perform small motor tasks related to dressing and feeding herself. To ensure her safety while Jackie was preparing food, we had to file down the points on knives. We had to purchase pens and tableware with large grips on them and plates with lips around the edges so she could pick up her food more easily, and we needed to put hot drinks in insulated mugs with covers to prevent Jackie from spilling hot liquids on herself. The neurology department couldn't find anything better than tizanidine for controlling the trembling symptoms that were a constant source of discomfort for Jackie. Once we reached the fifth and the sixth year, her doctors didn't recommend giving more than 8 mg a day because any more wouldn't relieve symptoms.

Another significant problem that Jackie experienced was the inability to completely empty her bladder when she urinated. Her neurologist determined that this could be the cause of her recurring urinary tract infections and referred her to a urogynecologist, Dr. Abraham Morse. Dr. Morse recommended that Jackie begin using catheterization as means to reduce the number of UTIs she was experiencing. Both Jackie and I learned how to insert a catheter into her bladder to empty the urine. Initially, Jackie was able to self-catheterize, and she did this once per day. She also needed to wear Poise pads to prevent accidents that could happen whenever she strained her stomach muscles, such as when transferring or laughing.

In order to maintain muscle strength for as long as possible, Jackie rode a stationary bicycle for as long as she could. She also had physical therapy, which provided her with various strengthening exercises and tools such as squeeze balls, soft putty, and Thera-Bands to use each day. The fact that she never seriously hurt herself when she fell is due in large part, we believe, to her strength, which is why exercise is so important!

In addition to the physical problems caused by OPCA, patients often experience psychological problems as well. These include depression, compulsive behavior, sleep disorders, etc. Jackie has taken Paxil throughout her illness to aid with depression and also Wellbutrin. Other drugs that gave too many side effects were Mirapex and Bethanechol as they caused edema, nausea, and dizziness, so she stopped taking those because she felt better without them.

## Year Two

In the second year of her illness, Jackie's condition declined at a much faster rate than her family and doctors expected. Her muscles became more rigid, her tremors worsened, her eyesight diminished, and her speech became slurred. Her neurologist ordered tizanidine (6 mg a day; a muscle relaxant to calm down the trembling). In the fifth year, it was moved to 8 mg a day

She had more and more difficulty with dressing, bathing, and toileting. She required assistance getting dressed and could only do so while in bed. She needed to use a bath safety chair in the shower because she could no longer take a bath. I had to take over her dental care because she was no longer able to hold her electric toothbrush or floss—even with Toothettes floss sticks. We placed a commode next to the bed to make toileting more convenient, especially in the middle of the night. Jackie was no longer able to get in and out of bed by herself due to the increased trembling and the fact that her right leg had become completely rigid and immobile. At first, we simply removed the wheels from the bed frame so the mattress would be at a height that was easier for Jackie to reach. We also placed a bedside support rail for Jackie to grip when she was being transferred.

Jackie also began voiding less and less on her own, and we needed to increase the number of catheterizations from one to three per day to keep her comfortable. We began using waterproof bed pads that lay atop the sheets to reduce the number of linen changes needed. Increasing the number of catheterizations cut down the amount of transfers needed between bed, commode, wheelchair, and toilet, but it also increased the risk of UTIs by introducing a foreign object (e.g., catheter tube) into the bladder. In other words, the cure could also be a cause of infection! We tried Ditropan to slow down the bladder spasms so we wouldn't have to catheterize so often. This worked quite well at reducing the number of catheterizations needed per day, but it dehydrated Jackie so much that the cure became worse than the disease because it caused dry stools and constipation. Then we were faced with the problem of softening and loosening the stool. We found that lactulose works well but can result in diarrhea when you least expect it. Then we needed to change bed pads, pajamas, and panties, and sometimes sheets. Too loose bowels increase the chance of UTIs, so we learned to use lactulose sparingly. Our best results in regulating Jackie's bowels came by using, on average, three ducosate sodium, two Senokot, and four tablespoons of Fruit-Eze per day. (Note: Usually this has to be adjusted each time a new medication is added, especially antibiotics). Each person is different, but this is what has worked for us. Jackie usually can move her bowels on her own, but sometimes she needs indexing to get started or finish. The main thing is to keep her as comfortable and pain free as possible. A good rapport with our pharmacists has been very helpful because they usually have a strong knowledge of how each drug works and have given us very good feedback on regulating Jackie's needs.

**Jackie in her second year of Ataxia, 2002**

Walking with the walker became increasingly difficult, and she started falling more and more often. She began spending a great deal of time in bed not only to keep herself from falling, but also she was exhausted from the huge amount of effort required to do everything. When she was no longer able to go up and down the three steps leading in and out of the house, we had to install a wheelchair ramp. This was essential for preventing Jackie from becoming homebound at this relatively early stage of the disease. We were fortunate to have a friend whose family had a wheelchair ramp that they no longer used and were happy to pass on to someone else who needed one. We could not use the whole thing because of the different layout needed, so I built the top part of the ramp using wooden deck materials and attached the preconstructed metal ramp for the bottom part. Portable wheelchair ramps also are available, which can be useful when visiting other people's homes.

We also had to acquire an electric wheelchair because Jackie was no longer strong enough to maneuver the manual wheelchair on her own. We chose a Jazzy 1113 because it was relatively small and could fit through our interior doorways easily. Having an electric wheelchair was a bonus that gave Jackie a small but much-needed dose of freedom because she could now go outside in the yard on her own and even take "walks" around the block with me if she felt up to it. But be careful when purchasing this expensive equipment: the average price from local medical equipment providers is $5,000. You can go on the Internet and get one for an average price of $3,000, but then you have to worry about shipping costs. We were able to achieve significant savings by purchasing the "floor model" from our local provider that was retrofitted to meet our needs.

As Jackie's need for assistance increased, I began to have some difficulty keeping up with all that needed to be done. Not only was I spending more time helping Jackie, but also I had taken over all of her share of work around the house. My elderly mother also lives with us, and although she requires minimal care, it was yet another responsibility for me. We contacted our local senior center to see what assistance might be available to people in our situation, and they referred us to the Worcester Area Council on Aging. After reviewing our situation, they determined that we were eligible for some services such as meals-on-wheels and housekeeping. At this point, Jackie was still able to feed herself using weighted forks and spoons and adaptive bowls, plates, and cups. Occasionally, Jackie would choke on her drinks, but it was not a significant concern. Since she could no longer prepare meals, we decided to begin using meals-on-wheels for both Jackie and my mother to provide me some relief from cooking in the evenings. We also tried the housekeeping services, but I eventually decided I would rather do this myself.

We found that applying for a home-based Medicaid waiver by reducing all Jackie's assets and enabled Jackie to receive a greater number of needed services at significantly lower cost to our family. The reason for this is that only Jackie's social security income is counted. Our nursing services are coordinated by Elder Services of Worcester, Massachusetts, which assigns a caseworker to Jackie and orders the nursing agency to send nurses, speech therapists, occupational therapists, home health aids, and even meals-on-wheels, if desired. Our services also include a Lifeline and respite care for me, the caregiver. It is vital for the caregiver to get some time off when providing 24/7 patient care. The reason these respite services are provided is that the government saves 80 to 90 percent compared to paying for nursing home care. Perhaps even more will be done in future years to allow seriously ill people to stay at home. I currently get three hours of respite care two days per week, and eight hours of respite care one other day of my choosing.

Another difficulty during that second year was that Jackie began having sleep disturbances. She would have very vivid dreams and nightmares and act out physically in her sleep. Behaviors such as talking, yelling, hitting, flailing, and pinching were common. She also developed insomnia and often would go an entire night without sleeping. Her neurologist started her on clonazepam (Klonopin), which successfully alleviated these symptoms.

When she was no longer able to catheterize herself due to the severity of her tremors (she could not void more than 10 percent of her urine on her own at this point), I, upon her request, became her primary caregiver. We have been in the fortunate position of being able to keep Jackie at home for the entire duration of her illness because I was retired when she became ill and was willing and able to care for her. However, I cannot emphasize enough the important roles that Elder Services and MassHealth (Massachusetts Medicaid program) have played in facilitating Jackie's home care.

## Years Three and Four

As Jackie's ataxia progressed into the third and fourth years, she became almost completely bedridden. The only times she would leave her bed during the day were for breakfast, dinner, bathing, toileting, and occasional outings. We invested in an electric hospital bed so she could sit up comfortably and change positions whenever needed/desired. Getting a change of position is essential for someone who is immobile. The electric bed also made transferring from bed to wheelchair/commode easier for us both. I requested a trapeze for over the bed, which was very useful in helping Jackie maintain grip and upper-body strength, improve her lung capacity making breathing easier and less lung rattle, and enjoy some welcome stretching. We installed a wall-mounted television stand at the foot of her bed and placed a small television/VCR combo, a DVD player, and a five-disc CD player—all with remote controls—in the bedroom to make her space more pleasant.

Over the years I have found that if you can control constipation and keep UTIs in check, then you will have a pretty good handle on this disease. For catheterizations, I used a standard six inches straight, FG 14 catheter tube and try to do no more procedures than five times a day. We used a new tube each time. Whenever a UTI is present, I usually use Levaquin as directed. Cipro is good, but patients taking Wellbutrin have gotten strokes while on Cipro, so that is our reason for using Levaquin. Also, *Serratia marcescens* is sensitive to Levaquin and seems to show up a lot whenever we suspect a UTI. *Serratia marcescens* is of concern due to its increasing number of cases, virulence, and increasing resistance to antibiotics.

It was becoming increasingly clear that if we wanted to keep Jackie at home, we were going to have to make some modifications to our house in order to care for her properly. We hired a contractor with significant experience in home remodeling for handicapped persons. Although we did not have a great deal of space to work with, we were able to add on a large handicapped bathroom with a roll-in shower, a raised toilet surrounded by grab bars on the walls, a utility sink for easy cleanup, and a laundry room. I installed a full-sized stackable washer and dryer so laundry wouldn't have to be done in the basement. This has been a real time-saver for me. We also added a two-car garage and a wheelchair ramp that leads from the new bathroom directly into the garage. This made leaving the house much easier for us, especially in inclement weather. Last but not least, we built a three-season porch that Jackie also can enter from the bathroom. Before that, she didn't really have any place to sit out in the yard because it's so hard to move a wheelchair on grass. Another adaptation that has been very helpful when taking Jackie out of the house is a handicap-equipped van. We purchased a Ford Windstar that was retrofitted for use with a wheelchair. However, we did need to upgrade Jackie's electric wheelchair in order to fit into the van's locking mechanism.

# Home Improvements

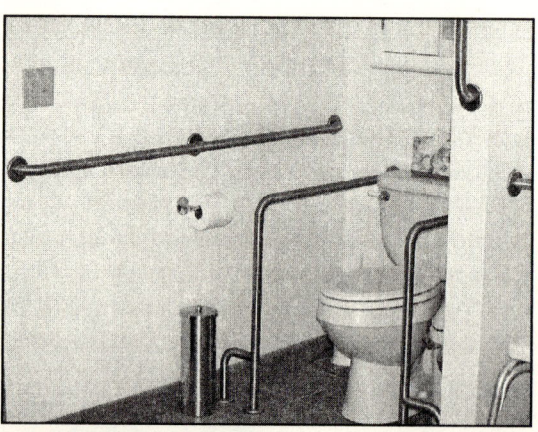

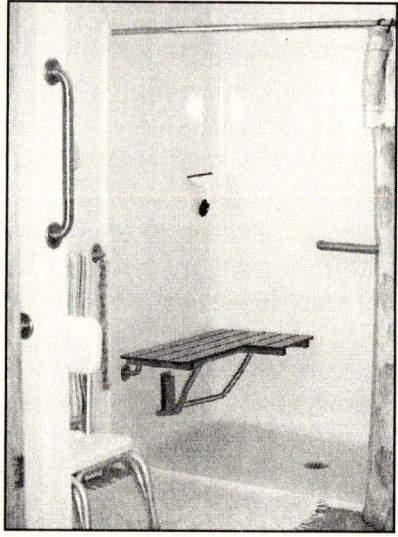

**Bathroom changes were made to improve ambulation**

## Home improvements (continued)

Screen Porch Added Off the Bathroom

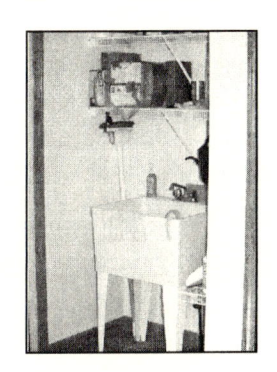

Utility Sink in the Bathroom

Remote Control Ceiling Fan

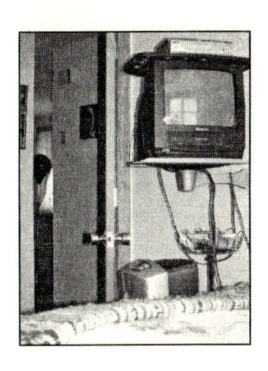

Remote Control TV

Stackable Washer/Dryer

Garage Wheelchair Ramp

Jackie experienced major loss of physical capability during this time period. Her speech worsened dramatically, and her legs became so rigid that she experienced a complete loss of dexterity. She could no longer walk with the walker, and she was not strong enough to hold on to the grab bars and hold/pull herself along. Jackie started wearing a gait belt around her waist, which is a strong locking canvas belt that I grasped to help her move from place to place. One that automatically opens with one touch is especially useful for mealtime because it can be loosened easily so as not to restrict breathing and then buckled back up again after eating without fumbling with the old buckle types. I continued to help Jackie walk by using the walker and gait belt to walk down the hallway to the kitchen for breakfast, as I believed that movement was still important. I also found tai chi to be very useful for me because it gives you good balance to aid in transferring an immobile patient.

Due to the fact that she could no longer dress herself and needed to be catheterized so frequently, she began wearing knee-length, short-sleeved nightgowns each day. We found that loose-fitting gowns are better than the perfect size. Headaches, which were present on and off from the beginning, increased in severity and occurrence but rarely required medication (Jackie used 1,000 mg. acetaminophen when needed). Dysphagia or difficulty swallowing started, and foods had to be cut into small pieces in order for Jackie to eat without choking.

## Years Five and Six

After five years, Jackie's ataxia has been retrograding so fast that it is almost impossible to keep up with it. I thought it had reached a worst-stage scenario after two years, but then each month or two, the retrograde would continue. All caregivers must be prepared for this decline as we have had to complete all the legal paperwork, such as power of attorney, health care proxy, last will and testament, do not resuscitate (DNR) forms, and affidavits signed by doctors, lawyers, and witnesses. As difficult as it is to know that Jackie wants no medical intervention to prolong her life, I will honor her request so as to not delay the inevitable.

Dysphagia is now a real problem. I have had to start pureeing all of Jackie's solid food and thickening all her drinks to the consistency of honey. These measures were needed not only to make it easier for Jackie to swallow, but also to stop any small pieces of food from wedging in the epiglottis or aspirating liquid, either of which might cause food to go into the lungs and cause pneumonia. I purchased a handheld mixer for a reasonable price at Wal-Mart, which is great for pureeing soft foods and for mixing thickener into juices and coffee. I also purchased an inexpensive food processor made by General Electric, which is great for pureeing dinner meals and works better than a blender. Jackie's speech therapists recommended sippy tips to put on straws, which makes it easy to take in liquid without the straw going too far into the palate. This saves a lot of choking and doesn't allow the patient to draw liquid too fast.

For large vitamins, Ester-C, cranberry pills, or acetaminophen, I use a simple mortar and pestle to grind them to dust. I add them to Jackie's pureed fruit, which makes it a lot easier for her to swallow. I purchased my mortar and pestle set at Bed and Bath for about twelve dollars. Most medications and supplements that are not timed-release can be crushed. I recommend doing this whenever swallowing is a problem.

Jackie has experienced a nearly total loss of speech, and she started speech therapy during this time period. A good speech therapist is most helpful for advice regarding equipment to aid the OPCA patient in communication. Jackie's therapist, Mary Ellen McClune, introduced a little electronic panel box with four large square buttons. We can program it with words to communicate whatever Jackie needs most, such as "bathroom," "pain," "catheterize," or just "yes" or "no." A second box was added with eight squares and a remote device, so Jackie does not have to reach for the buttons. We also had a book made up for Jackie that allows her to point to a square for many different subjects as well as letters to spell out words. Losing the ability to talk is the most difficult part of OPCA. Communication loss is most depressing for the patient at this stage of retrograde and even harder for the caregivers. Friends and family members are particularly affected because they become uncomfortable trying to carry on a one-sided conversation and get upset about not knowing what Jackie is trying to say.

Physically, Jackie is now totally bedridden except for occasional short trips to visit her neurologist, our son's family who lives close by, or the dairy for an ice cream. She has a total loss of movement in her right leg, and only 5 percent use of right arm. A hoyer lift is needed by caregivers in order to transfer her to the bathroom for showers. We invested in a high-end wheelchair that can recline and has a tray to allow her to sit comfortably when she is not in bed. Her primary care physician now comes to the house whenever Jackie has an appointment. Her failing health prompted us to start in-home hospice this past August. We have been very impressed with the quality of the hospice staff and the compassionate care they provide to Jackie as well as their attention to other household and family members. Hospice has been invaluable for providing medications and solutions to make Jackie more comfortable and my job easier. While we were reluctant about starting hospice, our doctors advised us to bring in hospice sooner rather than later, and our experience definitely supports their recommendations.

In order to give myself some much-needed extra sleep on weekends, I started using an indwelling catheter from Thursday to Sunday, which worked well for some time. But a recurring lower back injury has forced me to decrease the number of transfers made back and forth to the bathroom, so Jackie now has an indwelling catheter much of the time. We have been surprised by the relative lack of urinary tract infections versus the increase that we expected from leaving a catheter in place for two to three weeks (we were told that the chances of getting a urinary tract infection are tripled when using a Foley catheter). For us, it seems the risk of introducing bacteria with each catheterization is greater than that of leaving the catheter in place for an extended period of time. Jackie also has experienced more difficulty in moving her bowels and usually needs probing in order to fully evacuate. As recommended by the hospice nurse, we now leave a disposable paper-and-plastic pad under Jackie at all times so she can move her bowels whenever she has the urge.

A very disconcerting development is that the "lung crackle" in Jackie's upper chest has become much more prominent. Hospice provides us with hyoscyamine (Levsin) to help Jackie breathe more comfortably. We will use atropine when the chest congestion becomes worse. Often,

I give her chest percussion to loosen it up. The frustrating part of Jackie's ataxia is that she cannot expectorate, and most congestion is swallowed or excreted. She hardly has enough wind to blow her nose, and drooling and nasal oozing are always present at this stage. Mucinex is very good for keeping the lung congestion loose, but it may exacerbate choking if the patient cannot expectorate enough to suction.

# Part One: A Caregiver's Story

## FINAL COMMENTS

I have a problem with the middlemen who supply equipment for ataxia patients. They, along with some of the medical professionals, treat OPCA like any other brain ataxia. It is my belief that this disease retrogrades faster than all others, and therefore the patient needs specialty equipment a lot sooner. For example, by the time my wife got her special phone, she was hardly able to speak. And this was only four and a half years into the disease. The same goes for physical therapy—the sooner the better. To my wife's detriment, the insurance company kept discontinuing physical therapy—this is something the doctors should decide.

I also have a problem with the neurology department clinic that Jackie used in the early years of her disease. The doctors are very well qualified but are overwhelmed by hospital policy. Patient care at the neurology clinic is overshadowed by profit line and massive understaffing or what appears to be overbooking. We have waited up to two and three hours to get in and out of there. This makes me so disappointed for Jackie's sake, as she gets tired and sore after only an hour in the wheelchair. My other pet peeve is that it can take three to five days to receive a return phone call that is made for a good reason, such as adjusting medication. We have experienced other problems with parking. Large hospitals let healthy people compete with the handicapped for tickets and space. This is unacceptable in my opinion, and I hope the public will stop the hospital bureaucracy from treating them like cattle, especially when it's for the sick and dying.

Our hopes for the future are that the government will allow money to go where needed in stem cell research and gene study. They might not be capable of isolating a gene specifically for OPCA, but it may be possible to put it in a category where remedial action can be taken, if not to cure it, then maybe to slow or stop the retrograde. Our government is so caught up in catering to corporate lobbyists that they ignore the health care and social service needs of Americans. The best we can hope for is to not ever again put in such an ultra right-wing government that ignores the health of the general population and keeps running up huge deficits.

Our prayers and admiration reach out to all the doctors, nurses, therapists, social workers, and caregivers whose compassion and dedication help make life bearable for Jackie and me. We are most grateful to Dr. Ingrid Fuller, Jackie's primary care doctor, for her expertise, guidance, and support that she has given generously from day 1 of this disease. We also are grateful to Christen Mastrovito, for providing such valuable services at each stage of retrograde. A special thanks to Marie Davis, who is halfway through nursing school and has given Jackie and I much support. Her loving, compassionate care, and thoroughness have been a godsend. And heartfelt thanks to Drs. Paula Ravin and Abraham Morse for guiding us in the early years of this disease and giving so unselfishly their time and professional opinions.

# Part Two: A Caregiver's Story
# The Final Journey

In August of 2005, it was recommended by Jackie's primary care physician that she should start hospice sooner rather than later. When your patient has reached the stage of daily discomfort and retrograde, it will be quite obvious. At this point, Jackie couldn't talk or move very much, and we both knew we were entering the final phase of this disease. I was pureeing all her food, not just her dinner. It meant pureeing fresh fruit every morning and thickening all her juices and coffee, so we called in hospice for the final year of Jackie's life, although we had no idea she would leave us that soon. The good thing about hospice is that they provide relief for the caregiver as well. I was often elated that I on occasion could get a back massage on the same day it was provided for Jackie by a real guardian angel named June Bessette, who was also a nurse and member of the hospice team. Massage is a great way to relieve stress and tension. Also, hospice, through Elder Services of Worcester, Inc., allowed me respite care for an average of three days per week, four hours per day. This was the only way I was able to get my errands done or just take a few hours to myself to relax. Even with this time off, I still had to buy in large quantity to lessen the number of trips needed.

Shortly after calling in hospice, I was finally convinced to put an indwelling catheter on Jackie after almost six years of straight manual catheterization. This was a great relief in my schedule and allowed me more time to get other work done. I could never plan on when the next time Jackie had to void, so it helped greatly. Even with this change, it was still difficult to prevent more UTIs that would occur on an average of about every two months. I was quite surprised that urinary tract infections didn't appear more often since the general rule was that the bacteria could travel up the tube and exacerbate the UTI problem. Even with this change, it was unavoidable with an immobile patient that the UTIs would be back. It only takes a trace of fecal material to start an infection, and I was constantly giving her Levaquin for a few days at a time every four to six weeks just to control it, not to eradicate it. By doing it this way, she didn't become immune to the medication.

Hospice provides a comfort care package that contains drugs such as morphine, prochlorperazine (Compazine for nausea), scopolamine patches (controls secretion and drooling), anti-inflammatory rectal suppositories (acedaminefen), lorazepam, haloperidol, phenytoin, plus Bisac-Evac suppositories, and hyoscyamine to help with chest fluid.

**Ron and Jackie in her last year.**

Medications that we used on a steady basis right up to her last day:

1. Clonazepam (for sleep and comfort; last six months dose was moved up to 1 mg)
2. Tizanidine (4 mg)
3. Bupropion (150 mg)
4. Paroxetine (40 mg)
5. Aceminefen (two 500 mg tablets morning and night; pureed)
6. Sena tabs (dulcasate sodium)
7. Ranitidine (150 mg morning and dinner)
8. Mometasone furoate ointment (for dry patch outbreaks)
9. Levaquin (antibiotic as needed)
10. Clotrimazole (antifungal ointment to control rash)

It must be remembered that the comfort care box is only for emergencies, or if you're waiting for a prescription renewal to arrive and need a dose right away. I did on occasion use acetaminophen suppositories when Jackie was having trouble swallowing during some of the rare times that she would have a temperature. She didn't like to take acetaminophen liquid because the taste was awful. So the suppositories were a good way to solve that problem, and it got into the system fast without choking on pills. Of course you can always puree it, but it still leaves the patient one more thing to negotiate orally. So you constantly have to ask the patient what their pain level is and act accordingly.

One of the best pieces of information I can give to caregivers is on the comfort of an immobile patient that can't speak. It is very hard to recognize when they need something even to the smallest detail. So just imagine that you have a terrible itch and you can't scratch it. How horrible and uncomfortable is this for your patient who is relying on you to ease their problem. The most prevalent place on Jackie was her neck, ears, face (especially the eyebrows), and her head and shoulders, and sometimes the lower extremities. Every morning upon waking, I would empty her Foley bag and record the amount of void. Once this was done, I would start with a slow finger pressure along the spine and massage her back and neck. Please don't do the neck unless you have had special instruction. Simple passive motion left and right, side to side, and some mild forward movement gave her not only better head movement, but helped her open her mouth enough to get a spoon in her mouth. Also, some jaw-stretching exercises were very helpful in aiding her the ability to eat her breakfast. Then lastly, I would wash her qi. Washing the qi is the last step when finishing the art of Qigong. It is a slow hand rub from head to foot and back again and is very relaxing to your patient. I practice Qigong myself, and it's a nice way to complete an exercise, and it's called moving your chi. Qigong is actually the mother of tai chi, and a lot of the movements are incorporated from Qigong, especially deep breathing. So every morning Jackie would look quite peaceful and usually had a big smile for me. What a beautiful way for your patient to start the day. In fact, she smiled like that even on the final morning.

I don't think there is any way a caregiver can do a proper job if they don't keep some kind of daily record of procedure. I kept a simple loose-leaf notebook. On an hourly and daily basis, I would record urine voids, medicine given and how much, the dose and how often taken. Also, whenever there was any indication of a UTI, it would be there for referral. This way, I had an instant and reliable explanation for the many doctor and nurse inquiries. It's also a good idea to record the length of time between bowel movements so remedial action can be taken earlier rather than later if your patient is staying constipated for too long a time. If there has been no movement for three or four days, don't panic, it takes twice as long at this stage of retrograde. If your patient is having trickle in the four quadrants, it won't be long before movement is initiated. Suppositories can be used, but I never use one if there is no indication of stool.

In October 2005, we started giving Jackie two Tylenol with breakfast and at bedtime to help stabilize her comfort level. Her UTI was showing up almost on a monthly basis now, and I gave her an antibiotic as needed. Generally, her primary doctor, Ingrid Fuller, wanted to stay with a dose for one or two days just to control the bacteria, not eradicate it. Usually we could stay UTI-free four to six weeks on average. By doing it this way, she didn't become immune to the antibiotic.

As Jackie needed more medications, her nurse would make that recommendation to us and then have the primary doctor approve it. So we started giving her hyoscyamine to keep the chest rattle clear and make her breathing easier. And with each new medication, I usually had to adjust her stool softeners accordingly as she was drinking less and less, which just added to the problem. I could tell just by reading her urine output each morning whether or not her bowel movements would be dry or normal. If each morning there was less than 800 cc in her Foley indwelling bag, we knew that it would take longer to move. I would record the volume of each movement and how often in order to not let her get compacted. That would be the worst thing that could happen, especially when the patient has so many other side effects.

Time was moving so fast I had all I could do to shop for Christmas presents and make it as normal as possible for her. A lot of the gifts I purchased were through the Internet and catalogues. On Christmas day, I brought her out in the living room so she could see the tree and the presents. I of course opened each one for her, and she smiled and slept off and on. We knew she was rapidly retrograding, and it broke my heart as I became very depressed at this stage of her illness. She loved being in the living room or screen porch, which helped get away from that four-wall syndrome. Little did I know she would only live for nine more months.

## January, February, and March 2006

An amazing thing about Jackie's illness was that her blood pressure was always in a good range right up to the last days. Except for a few headaches and general discomfort, she remained pain-free until her demise. I did have to constantly monitor her temperature and watch her urine very closely, and after a while, I could tell just by looking at her voids if bacteria was building up to high. I didn't even have to have it analyzed to know it most likely was *Serratia*. I would give her Levaquin as needed according to her primary doctor's recommendations, and she would stay UTI-free for another four to six weeks.

As retrograde continued, her dysphagia became more problematic in her ability to swallow all of her food without having one-third of it in around her teeth, plate, and palate even when it was pureed like baby food. So in-between and at the end of each meal, I would use Toothettes (sponge on a stick) to clean around teeth and gums; and after dinner, I would thoroughly brush her teeth with an electric toothbrush. I also used a suction pump, as needed, to prevent any backfall into the palate and throat.

We often take it for granted that our food will always have variety and be tasty and different. But when a patient is eating puree for all three meals, it becomes boring, and all foods taste the same. So any alternative you can give the patient brings them great joy even for the smallest change in menu. Protein drinks and ice cream were big favorites of Jackie's. I used to bake homemade squash bread, puree it and put whipped topping on it. That was one of her favorites in the morning. Other items she liked include strawberry shortcake, mousse, hot fudge sundaes, ice-cream sodas, puddings, and homemade chocolate cream pie (pureed crust). These dessert choices are also a great way to add medicine when needed and off-set any sour tasting medications. I always gave her ice cream with her nighttime medication, and it always put a smile on her face. And she usually went to sleep in ten minutes.

At this stage of her illness, I had to start giving her lactulose on a steady basis to counteract the hyoscyamine, which not only dries up the lung mucus, but also dries up the stools. It is quite a job to balance normal movement, especially when your patient loses the muscular strength to move on his or her own. You can do one of two things here. You can raise the dose of lactulose, Fruit-Eze, and dulcasate sodium and deal with diarrhea or use just enough lactulose to keep the stools soft and index your patient. Over the years, I found this latter method to reduce the frequency of UTIs. I also have a bulging disc at L4 and L5, which is one of the main reasons for using chuckers more often than bathroom transfers—which often left Jackie exhausted. So each caregiver has to do what works best for all concerned. Ongoing back pain was a constant problem because my body never had enough sleep or downtime to recover from an already-existing condition. But I was supermotivated to honor her request for me to be her caregiver, and I seldom showed her that I was in constant pain.

## April, May, and June 2006

With six months to go, I'm adding even more lactulose to her diet because Jackie is starting to drink less and sleep more during the day, and it's not unusual now for her to go as much as three to five days without movements. In order to hydrate her, we had to constantly give her small amounts of liquid every fifteen minutes. Her breakfast is almost nonexistent except for a little cream of wheat and juice. Lunch is usually pureed fruit drinks or protein drinks and sherbet, which helps to hydrate.

Voids were getting less and less as 400 cc is her average twenty-four-hour output, and she was having a lot of trouble trying to just have enough strength to sip a drink. What amazed me was the courage to keep on going as every day she would look at me and smile. I knew she was saying I love you even though she couldn't speak. She could squeeze my fingers just enough to feel pressure, and she would communicate by blinking as well. You would be surprised at the conversations we had with just yesses and noes. I could almost tell just the way she looked at me if she was uncomfortable or needed something.

Approaching the last three months, Jackie still tried to do her daily crosswords from the newspaper. By now she couldn't hold her pen, but she still liked to look at it and try to scribble. It was so pathetic to watch, and I usually assisted her the best I could. She would tire and sleep in between and then watch *General Hospital* or *Oprah* on television.

Ron and Jackie about five months before her passing (2006).

As her inability to eat or drink worsened, it became problematic to control dryness. Less liquid intake meant adding more and more lactulose to her now-skimpy diet and more pureed prune, fig, and date mixture as well. We didn't want to run the chance of her getting impacted, and that would be most uncomfortable for an immobile patient. Of course the problem is constantly being exacerbated from the medication to keep her lungs from filling up with mucus. We tried every way possible to hydrate. Sherbet, popsicles, and juices were the mainstay, but I had to slowly pump the pureed liquids into her mouth as she was losing the ability to draw on the straws. The special cups we used had rubber tops, which when squeezed would suction the liquid up into the straw, and all the patient had to do was swallow. They also have a piece that attaches to the bottom of the straw, so when you suck on straw, the liquid won't go back down when you stop sipping. This was great for Jackie through most of her dysphagia as she would not get as tired when drinking. Still with about three months left, we only had to give two 500 mg of acetaminophen every night on average. I was depressed daily about her ataxia but elated that she was relatively pain free at this late stage.

Each day now, I noticed Jackie slowly losing her appetite even more as she was only eating about one-third of dinner and not even drinking her morning coffee anymore. July was a fairly good month for Jackie, and I would take her for ice cream whenever she felt strong enough. Even though the battery might go dead with an existing problem with our handicap van, as explained later in this book, I felt it was more important to get her out of the house. These trips were getting few and far between now. Even though she was getting reluctant to leave her room, I still felt it was good for her to get away from that four-wall syndrome.

Her lungs were getting more and more problematic as I would often try to suction the mucus, but Jackie couldn't cough it up high enough for the suction tube to remove it. She just didn't have the strength, and a smart caregiver would never put the tube into the lungs for fear of infection. Putting Jackie on her side was the best way to calm the rattle, but she didn't like being on her side.

## Last Two Months

At this time, based on her difficulty breathing, the hospice nurses and primary doctor said to start giving Jackie morphine as needed. We also started her on oxygen twenty-four hours a day instead of intermittent use, and this helped make her more comfortable. But the low intake of food and drink was delaying her movements even longer. Seven to ten days were becoming the norm. This made me more apprehensive as it was clear that she was rapidly retrograding.

On August 5, hospice advised putting 1.5 mg scopolamine patches on her neck. These patches, which are medicine that is absorbed through the skin, help the patient breathe easier and are placed on the neck just behind the lower ear. Her breathing got better, and we continued using them right to the end. As her breathing got more and more difficult, I was instructed to put two patches on and change them every three days at the same hour each time. However, we would later have to stop using hyoscyamine because it was causing cross action with the patches, and this brought us to using the patches only.

From time to time, I began giving Jackie morphine as her chest pain warranted. The morphine relaxes the chest muscles and makes breathing easier and helps the patient rest or get more sleep. It, like any new added medication, would affect her regulation, and I was now dealing with ten days between movements. That really worried me as I was coming into

Jackie

a new territory with the final symptoms and was a little apprehensive to do my normal routine without consulting with the nursing department. So I increased her lactulose even more, but at this stage, there were only quarter movements, and I never knew when the next need would occur. It was bothersome because we had been so regulated, time wise, all through this sporadic disease.

It was at this time Jackie's lungs became so bad I strongly suspected pneumonia. Her temperature was running about 100 degrees and would shoot up to almost 102. I called the Hospice Team and got directions to start her immediately on 650 mg of APAP suppository (acetaminophen) to bring that temperature down. Also, I had to give her morphine 8:00 a.m., noon, 4:00 p.m., and 8:00 p.m. The primary doctor gave me a choice of giving her an antibiotic or just letting the disease run its course because the norm is it is only a temporary delay to the inevitable. However, as a caregiver, you do everything possible to keep your patient alive, so I explained to Jackie the situation and asked her if she wanted me to give her an antibiotic and that it was her choice. She blinked her eye to indicate yes. I said, "Are you sure?" She blinked her left eye, which meant yes, and squeezed my thumb to indicate okay with a big smile. Even though Jackie insisted on a DNR, she still was a battler right to the end.

I started her on an antibiotic for ten days, and much to my amazement, she started improving after only five days. During this time, I was using oxygen on a twenty-four-hour basis and would continue using it until her demise. This was the hardest I ever worked as a caregiver, as I didn't get hardly any sleep for three or four days in a row. Somehow, God gives you the strength to keep going. Her primary doctor was correct because it was only about a week, and Jackie start slipping back as expected. But I wouldn't be able to live with myself if I didn't follow her wishes.

Oxygen machines are very noisy, and for that reason come with a forty-foot tube. I kept the machine out on our enclosed screen porch about thirty feet away and could close the porch door and our bedroom door. This cut the noise down so it could hardly be heard. The companies that supply oxygen have tiny ear guards to protect skin breakdown around the ears that support the nose tube—just ask for them. If these ear holders aren't constantly monitored, you can hurt your patient as well as lose oxygen supply if it falls away. Also, you can buy ointment at any pharmacy to protect the inside of the patient's nostrils. It's a good idea as well to watch the strength of oxygen, so it doesn't make a nosebleed.

All in all, Jackie was comfortable in August except that she started getting bedsores on her buttocks. The constant use of her electric bed going up and down eventually broke the skin down. Also, it was an indication to me that her ability to heal was greatly diminished. She was rapidly losing a long and hard-fought battle, and I knew we didn't have much time left. Turning her on her side was the best way to take pressure off the buttocks, and it also made her breathe easier, but she just didn't like that position.

Jackie had a real valiant comeback from her pneumonia and felt so good I thought she was actually getting better. She ate better and drank better for about a week. Then the ataxia started its unrelenting retrograde again, and coming into September, she was losing the fight so fast I could hardly keep up with her care. On average, I was awake every two to three hours. Sleep deprivation weighed heavily on my body, and I prayed daily to God to give me the strength to honor her request—never to die in a nursing home or hospital. She would get her wish.

## The Last Month

September became the hardest month of all the six and three quarter years of caring for my angel. I was in constant touch with the hospice nursing department, and Jackie's nurse, Anne Ancona, who was my lifeline to succeed in keeping Jackie free of any undue pain. Also, Pam Rososky, Jackie's certified home health aid was the best I have ever seen in patient daily care. I was very blessed to have these outstanding hospice workers caring for Jackie. Surely they are doing God's work. When it comes to giving out Oscars and other awards, the real people that should receive a trophy for their accomplishments are the hospice workers.

Pam

Anne

Pamela (Jackie's talented Certified Home Health Aide),
Jackie, and Nurse Anne Ancona.

I started to give Jackie morphine on a daily basis; two to three times during the day and night respectively as needed, as her comfort level required it almost on an hourly basis. I began leaving her oxygen on twenty-four hours a day also, but took it off for short periods to rest her nasal passages and just to make her more comfortable. She started to sleep almost all day now, and her eating was down to about 10 percent for the day.

I have no doubt in my mind, looking back, during this last month that God had literally taken control of my body and directed it to complete my task. For my body and mind were completely burned out. It was only a month after Jackie left that the benefits of more sleep improved my bulging disc at L4 and L5, and I was able to start doing my activities again. I couldn't believe it.

# The following is a printout of some of my notes taken during Jackie's last month:

| Date | Dinner | ML Voided (per 24 Hr) | Mucous | Bowels/ Day | Temp (as Needed) | Oxygen am/pm | Acetaminophen (am / pm) | Lactulose am.p m | Fluconazole (Yeast) | Levaquin | Hyoscyomine am/pm | Morphine |
|---|---|---|---|---|---|---|---|---|---|---|---|---|
| 9/1/06 | 8-Jan | 450 | * | 0 | * | yes | 2/2 | 1/1 | | | | |
| 9/2/06 | 2/3 | 400 | * | 0 | * | no/yes | 2/2 | 1/1 | | | | |
| 9/3/06 | 1/4 | 450 | | 1/4th | * | no/yes | 2/2 | 1/0 | | | | |
| 9/4/06 | 1/3 | 300 | | full | * | All day | 2/2 | 1/0 | | | | |
| 9/5/06 | 1/3 | 400 | | full | * | All day | 2/2 | 0/1 | | | | |
| 9/6/06 | 1/2 | 400 | | half | * | no/yes | 2/2 | 1/0 | | | | |
| 9/7/06 | 1/8 | 350 | | 0 | | All day | 2/2 | 0/0 | | | | |
| 9/8/06 | 1/3 | 300 | | 0 | | All day | 2/2 | 1/1 | 1 | | | |
| 9/9/06 | 1/3 | 300 | | full | | All day | 2/2 | 1/1 | | | | |
| 9/10/06 | 1/3 | 375 | | 0 | | All day | 2/2 | 1/0 | | | | |
| 9/11/06 | 1/3 | 300 | | 0 | | All day | 2/2 | 0/0 | | | | |
| 9/12/06 | 1/4 | 350 | | full | | All day | 2/2 | 3 Tsp | | | | |
| 9/13/06 | 1/4 | 395 | | 0 | | All day | 2/2 | 2/0 | | | | |
| 9/14/06 | 1/8 | 300 | | 0 | | All day | 2/2 | 1/0 | | | | |
| 9/15/06 | 1/3 | 350 | * | 0 | | All day | 2/2 | 2/0 | | | | |
| 9/16/06 | 1/4 | 250 | | 0 | | All day | 2/2 | 2/0 | | | | |
| 9/17/06 | 1/8 | 350 | | full | | All day | 2/2 | 2/0 | | | | |
| 9/18/06 | 1/2 | 320 | | 0 | | All day | 2/2 | 2/0 | | | | |
| 9/19/06 | 1/4 | 300 | | 0 | | All day | 2/2 | 2/0 | | | | |
| 9/20/06 | 1/4 | 300 | | 0 | | All day | 2/2 | 2/0 | | | | |
| 9/21/06 | 3 TBLSP | 200 | | little | | no/yes | 2/2 | 2/0 | | 1 | | |
| 9/22/06 | 1/3 | 300 | | full | | no/yes | 2/2 | 2/0 | | 1 | | |
| 9/23/06 | 1/3 | 300 | | 0 | 98 am-97.1 | no/yes | | 2/0 | | 1 | 1 | |
| 9/24/06 | 1/3 | 300 | | 1 fourth | 97 | All day | | 2/0 | | 1 | 1 | 6:30pm |
| 9/25/06 | 1/4 | 325 | | 0 | 98 | All day | | 2/0 | | | 1 | 6:00pm |
| 9/26/06 | 1/8 | 325 | | 0 | 98 | All day | | 0/0 | | | 1/1 | 7:05pm 5:00am |
| 9/27/06 | 0 | 300 | | 0 | 8 | All day | | 0/0 | | | 1/3 | 12:20pm 1:20 pm 4:45 pm 8:45 pm 1:00 am |
| 9/28/06 | 0 | 350 | | 0 | 98 at 12:00pm; 103.5 at 10:00pm; 101.1 at 4:45am | All day | | 0/0 | | | 1 @ 10:30 am 2 @ 4:00 am | 8:15am 11:45 am 3:30 pm 6:10 pm 9:00 pm 3:45 am 4:15 am |
| 9/29/06 | 0 | | | | | Until ToD | | 0/0 | | | 1 @ 10:30 am 1 @ 12:00 pm | 7:00 am 8:30pm |

8:35 am, patient stopped breathing, 9:0 am pronounced dead

# Part Three: A Caregiver's Story
# Grievance

For almost seven years in my private moments, I would cry for my lifelong partner on a daily basis. It was that sad of a disease. Little did I know that the grievance would be at its worst several months after she died. Long illnesses are very hard on the caregiver because even though you know it's the disease that took your loved one, you still feel responsible that she could have been kept alive longer.

Fortunately, the hospice programs in Massachusetts are set up to have extensive follow-up with group or individual counseling as well as ongoing literature to help cope with the loss of your loved one. Three months after Jackie died, I reached a peak of depression and I didn't feel I was coming down off of a variety of physical and emotional side effects, such as high systolic blood pressure, confusion, anger, forgetfulness, and a general tired feeling. So after discussing my problems with Janet Mullin, hospice manager for University of Massachusetts Medical Center, I called in a hospice grievance counselor named Carol Sazama a member of my wife's hospice team who had 20 years' experience and she helped me considerably. I had three sessions with her over the course of about five weeks. I was told to write letters to my wife and how I felt before she died and right at death. If you write about the last hour of death and read it over and over, the brain will slowly wash the pain from memory like slowly peeling an onion skin away until there is nothing left. So I can't stress enough the need to not take grievance lightly. I thought I would not have any problems on that end because of my being so close to this ataxia for almost seven years. I thought that the hardest part was seeing my wife die by my side and in my arms. No, the hardest part was facing life without her in which I could never remember ever feeling so lonely and depressed.

So I was asked to keep a journal and write my thoughts down on paper, like topical—what do I think of death? What do I imagine it will be like? Second, letters to Jackie—share my feelings and emotions. Check in—what emotions am I feeling specifically? What triggered them? How can I normalize my feelings with regard to what I know about? And what do I need now to feel better?

**Here are a few samples of some of these letters I wrote to my dead wife:**

**Dear Jackie,**

The natural process of living is dying, so death is inevitable. Sometimes the fear of how much pain I will have at the end of my journey comes to mind every once in a while, but I don't dwell on it. Maybe when you get to be a senior citizen you think about it more often, especially after seeing you slowly retrograde and die. When you passed it left quite an impression on me because of your difficulty to breathe during the last 48 hrs. You were heaving and struggling for air. It was at this time I started giving you morphine more often as needed and it calmed your breathing right down and you looked peaceful. Your eyes opened and looked at me a minute before your beautiful spirit left the room. It was like a huge vacuum that quickly released it's grip. At first I thought you were just sleeping because your body stayed warm for at least 20 minutes, before gradually going cold. I closed your eyes and then I knew you had left. I felt like my heart went with you and I knew my life would never be the same. I guess it is true that only the good die young.

With that being said I truly believe your spirit moved to a higher dimension and not very far away. So, I'm not afraid of death and I feel we will meet again soon. Just like the movie "The Gladiator" when they say-" We Will Meet Again Soon, But, Not Yet, Not Just Yet". I imagine death will be just like falling asleep. If you don't wake up then you will never have to worry about it.

**Dear Jackie,**

I pray every day that you are at peace and I know your spirit dwells amongst us. Life without you has been a bit of a struggle lately, but I know in time the pain will lessen.

I remember all the quality times we shared together and I was honored to be your caregiver for the last 7 years. I believe God was with me every step of the way guiding me so I wouldn't make any mistakes in caring for one of his angels. I'm consoled that there was plenty of time to tell you how much you meant to me and what a very special person you were to me and our children. You were a great Mother, wife, and home maker. You were my guardian angel for almost 46 yrs. and God allowed me to be yours all during that horrible disease which took you on your journey much too early. I am stronger and a better person for having known you. You have left a legacy unmatched by anyone. I love you and will never forget you even as I let you go, you will always be a part of me.

**Dear Jackie,**

You are on my mind every day. I pray for you on a daily basis. I think of all the good times we had at Cape Cod, walking the beaches, eating out at all those good restaurants, and especially when on the fitness trail. Do you remember me taking your picture in the second year of your illness? You were hanging on the rings and lifting yourself off the wheelchair. We even walked a half mile with you using your walker. Most of all getting those ice-cream sundaes at the School House was a special treat. At least that was one thing you could enjoy even with your disphagia.

I read in the book that the Hospice counselor gave me the following: "Sometimes in my darkness I believe I'm held in a love which supports all creation, not always but sometimes." Those were some pretty powerful words. I can remember many times during your care, of having the most profound feeling of peace of mind and joy that I have ever experienced. Could it be that I tapped into that universal energy which many people think of as divine? Anyway, I know it was that kind of love and peace you gave to your whole family and your loving spirit will always be with us.

Since your passing every time I hear Martina McBride sing "In My Daughter's Eyes," or "In God's Will," I cry for you because I know how much those songs meant to you in your last months and the special relationship you had with our oldest daughter that was reflected in the song "In My Daughter' Eyes."

**Dear Jackie:**

Having no one to talk to is a big loss, especially after 46 years with the same person. The ability to just hold hands is gone forever. It's like being left alone on an island. I feel like I'm on Walden Pond.

My grief counselor asked me to write what my thoughts were upon administering morphine to you in your last hour. So I wrote that I had a strong feeling that you were suffering. I asked you if you needed more morphine. You squeezed my finger for yes, and I knew you had a 10 mg dose an hour earlier, but my fear of you being in agony that last 5 minutes made me know I was doing the right thing for you. You had complete faith in my decisions. I knew you were in God's hands and I was aware that this was the first time I gave you morphine only 1 hour after the last dose and instinctively knew you were at the end. A few minutes later you struggled to look at me and that was your way of saying goodbye. I cry with great emotion writing this. It was very painful. But, I know I did everything humanly possible to keep you pain free. I know that God guided me every step of the way to give me the strength to finish the job. But, I keep wondering if you know that now?

**Dear Jackie:**

I'm asked a second time what my emotions are after morphine was given to you and how I feel just starting this letter.

I feel directions for dosage given by Hospice were followed explicitly by the caregiver. I know you had the very best of care in which I am very proud of. I feel remorse on a daily basis, but with less impact. I'm able to go about my daily routine, but not without some anger, and confusion now and then.

**Dear Jackie:**

I keep thinking back to Sept. 29, 2006 at 8.30 am. Not too long before you left us, I gave you what turned out to be, your last dose of morphine. Your heaving chest and difficult breathing were hard to bear even though I know you were not in pain.

Pamela arrived 2 min. before you left and said "Oh My God she waited for me to arrive before leaving us". I felt your body for a while and it stayed warm for what felt like an eternity leaving me some doubt weather you really did die. But, Pam said, Ron, She's dead. I gently closed your eyes and said my final good bye to you my beautiful angel. A part of me left with you. Shortly after you left us, Anne Ancona, your very talented nurse, told me to get a chair and sit beside you, hold your hand, and face the reality of your demise. That was really hard to do, but necessary to realize the end had come and the start of a deep wound that can only be healed with time. And, my dear it goes without saying that I can not keep my grievance inside or it can destroy me mentally and physically. The worst thing that one can do is internalize grief. It is so important to talk about the loss of a loved one even if it makes other people uncomfortable. So, my dear I will grieve for you for as long as it takes. Some day I will have to let you go. But of course I will never forget you or all the love we once shared.

**Dear Jackie,**

How are you? Where ever that is I hope it is peaceful and beautiful.

Today was a typical one. I put up a clothes rack in the hallway of my office and stained it in the afternoon. Went to Bed and Bath and bought a boot tray, floor mat for the back door to wipe off muddy shoes, and a shower curtain for the guest bathroom.

For dinner I made some lamb patties with fresh summer squash, and heated some left over home made American Chop Suey for a starch. It tasted great.

Later I watched "The Kingdom of Heaven" which was a very good movie showing the struggle between the Christians and Muslims over Jerusalem. That pretty much ended my day. I love you and pray for you every night. I pray also that God will give me the strength to carry on in your absence. You are gone but not forgotten.

**Dear Jackie,**

Today was a quiet Sunday and was quite relaxing. Did my usual exercises and then went for a mile walk at the park on this very warm day in January only about 3 months after your demise. Came back, showered, ate breakfast and then did the Sunday crossword. I think of you every time I do the crossword knowing how much you used to like to do them on a daily basis.

I worked outside in the yard for a while and walked out back to see if your hibiscus plant was still living. It looked wilted. I remember the day you said to plant it and it wasn't long before it started blooming. What beautiful flowers they are. I recall how I used to go out and wave to you while you were sitting in your lounge chair with Pauline Lebel eating dinner. You would immediately give me that great big smile and I can still see the joy on your face whenever I came back in and put a beautiful hibiscus rose flower on the tray of your lounge chair. In fact I still look at the macro shots with joy. Some day I will enlarge them to eight by tens, because they remind me of how pleased you were when ever a new bloom would appear. Unfortunately the frost got to this plant but, not before getting some nice macro pics that I will always treasure. (Note) Three months before Jackie died, my son brought over a hibiscus plant for her and it was so beautiful. It lasted about a month before losing all it's flowers and I thought it was dead. I was going to throw it away and Jackie kept blinking her right eye at me which meant no. So I slowly communicated with her that she wanted me to plant it outside which I did. That plant lasted until the frost got to it, but not before giving so many beautiful flowers for her to see and smell at dinner hour.

Jackie's favorite hibiscus flower.

**Dear Jackie,**

I just read that healing is impossible in loneliness and that conviviality is healing. I think this is true because I always feel better after being with people. But the reality of grief is you have to spend time alone and with time we shall heal the pain of your loss.

I stopped at your gravesight this afternoon and I prayed for you. I thought about when I have come to the end of the road and the sun has set for me, I want no rites in a gloom filled room, why cry for a soul set free? Miss me a little, but not too long, and not with your head hung low. Remember the love we once shared, miss me, but let me go. That's all I can remember of your service verses by an unknown author, but it has helped me a lot during this grieving process. And I know by writing your story it will help a lot other people and give you the legacy you were so proud of when the first part of your Care Giver's story appeared in the National Ataxia Foundation quarterly publication called "Generations".

With all our technology, we still don't know why men seek external power and listen to their personalities instead of their souls. We practice genocide on our own species as well as the animal kingdom. We tell our children to "don't lie, don't cheat, don't steal," but when they grow up and go into business, that's just what they will do. For instance, take professional wrestling. This is a disgrace in which young impressionable minds keep having their fight or flight patterns interrupted with threats, verbal abuse, bad language, and probably why the United States produces more serial killers than the rest of the whole world put together.

Our prisons are being filled up with men and women that go into a sentence and come out worse than when they went in. Then when they get out, they perpetrate even worst crimes. Our jobs have been sent overseas, and our economy has been devastated from state to state. Worst of all, these companies are rewarded with tax incentives and allowed to keep the bulk of their money outside of America to avoid paying taxes.

## Some Last Thoughts

One of the things that really bothered me during Jackie's illness was the equipment providers. There isn't, in my opinion, enough oversight and reprimand to some of the disingenuous health servers who could care less if they are gouging the sick and dying. As far as I know, there is no one in the government to oversee prices or safety of what they sell. Some stores won't even sell you equipment if it is billed through MassHealth (Medicaid). They say it is too much paperwork. Some companies send a shower chair and have no idea whether or not it is safe to transfer a patient onto. I had to return two folding shower chairs because I was afraid they would collapse. Another local provider sent me a shower chair with brakes that didn't work. When I tried to have them send new wheels, they decided to just take the chair back and forget the whole sale. I am certain they will sell this chair to another customer. Another example was when I purchased a new high-end lounge chair for Jackie for $1,200 dollars, and it needed a plastic tray. The tray was a simple plastic one like you see on a baby high chair. The provider wanted $300 for the tray. After some painful negotiations, I worked the salesman down to $150. That tray should have come with the lounge chair, but they try to squeeze every ounce of money they can out of you. It's like dealing with a used-car salesman. This is an area of health care that badly needs oversight by a reliable source in the government, and the sooner the better.

One of the smallest but most painful events that happened to me was having to deal with Social Security's giving my wife her check for September and taking it back six weeks after Jackie died. Because Jackie died on September 29, one day short of a full month, her check was electronically grabbed right out of our checking account because of a 1938 law that gives them the right. The law states that anyone receiving a check during the month they die must give it back. The reason this bothered me so much is when you are grieving, this is like a slap in the face, especially when the government saved hundreds of thousands of dollars by my caring for Jackie at home. It is my opinion that Jackie should have been able to keep twenty-nine days of that check. I was told by my local congressmen and women I would get the check back but was later told that because of the 1938 law, there wasn't anything they could do. This law needs to be changed as well as a law to prevent our government from stealing money from the Social Security fund and spend more money than they are receiving.

Lastly, the most painful event during Jackie's illness was the trauma she and I went through with buying and converting a Ford Windstar to a handicap van. This van had a constant draw on the battery, and to this day, the problem hasn't been fully diagnosed or repaired. And both service departments at Ford and Adaptive Mobility said they could not find a problem, even though they kept replacing the batteries.

On August 6, 2003, I purchased a Ford Windstar from the then Duddie Ford through my then salesman in Westborough, MA. This vehicle would be adapted to a handicap van by Ford provider Adaptive Mobility, located at 15 Fall River Avenue, Seekonk, Massachusetts. Adaptive Mobility has a parent company in New Mexico where my van was allegedly sent for the following adaptive changes:

1. The van was to have a tow package and wiring for trailoring installed. There was never any mention that the original backup light harness would be removed by Adaptive Mobility.
2. The van would take four to six weeks to be adapted to a handicap van. The work would be done in New Mexico. It was my understanding the vehicle would be transported so no extra mileage would be put on my new vehicle.
3. A PIN (personal identification number) would be used to discount the price.
4. Original measurements for Jackie's Jazzy 1113 electric wheelchair were taken by Mr. Nicholas, and that the EZ Lock system would be adapted to it. (Note: When the van came back for delivery, my salesman said we would have to buy a new wheelchair even though the van was purchased and measured for the old chair. Adaptive Mobility wanted three thousand dollars. I agreed to only pay one thousand dollars more in order not to delay delivery any longer than necessary as my dying wife had already been kept waiting four months longer than necessary.)

## Jackie

After the first purchase of the van and down payment, I was told by my salesman, that my vehicle was sold to another customer by another salesman. I was shocked beyond belief, especially when they said I would have to buy another vehicle instead of giving the original purchase back to me. This set us back by two more weeks. Then conversion and delivery was promised in four to six weeks. It took four months to get the second new van back. After numerous calls, my salesman said the delay was because by by using a PIN number he had to go for cheaper transportation since he lost so much money on the rebate PIN. When the van left to have conversion, it had fifteen miles on it. It came back with over two hundred miles on it. And for each time the service department had the vehicle, they would then drive it to Adaptive Mobility, which kept adding two hundred more miles each time it had to be serviced to find what caused a constant draw on my battery. Ford Service Department, now owned by Herb Chambers, said there was nothing wrong with the van. After the warrantee was expired on the van, I took it to two other companies to install wiring, and both said the problem was with Ford and their provider Adaptive Mobility. So one company stripped down the van and checked all the wiring. They found that my Windstar has a constant 1.4 to 1.7 amp draw on the battery. So it was only a matter of weeks before the battery would keep going dead and caused so many traumas for me and Jackie during the worst part of her health. I can't tell you what a broken heart I had at having to tell Jackie I couldn't even take her for an ice cream, never mind the numerous doctor appointments, and physical therapy that had to be cancelled.

At the present time even as I write this, Ford knows about the problem, and I am waiting to hear if they will take the vehicle back.

Numerous letters that I have written have never been answered. So I can't tell the reader how much mental torture it was to have a forty-seven-thousand-dollar vehicle fail so often. Somehow, I must find closure on this issue as I constantly have insomnia and keep dreaming about all the pain this caused Jackie and me on a daily basis.

Up to this printing, Ford has stated no responsibility and advises dealing with Adaptive Mobility only, even though it is one of their providers, who they contracted with to do handicap renovations.

I will have to take a huge financial loss on this van as I, in good conscience, could not sell and pass this van on to another family in need of a handicap vehicle.

*Update (April 28, 2008):* Not quite ready to take the loss on my van, I contacted the attorney general's office in Boston, Massachusetts, and gave them details on which my son-in-law says was quite a long and sordid story. The Boston office referred me to the Worcester Consumer Protection Service, and I spoke with a Michael Lombardi, who is located at the Molly Bish Center at Anna Maria College. Mr. Lombardi sent me a consumer complaint form to fill out, describing the problem and what I expected from the dealer. After sending the form to Mr. Lombardi, he sent it to Herb Chambers Ford in Westborough, Massachusetts, and a copy to Adaptive Mobility. Herb Chambers never answered this request, but Adaptive Mobility did, and this is what they said:

Dear Michael,

In reference to Mr. Lombard's claims in his consumer complaint form Adaptive Mobility Equipment, Inc. has no liability in this case. There are two key factors here the first being that the warranty was over on the conversion when this was brought to our attention. The second is that adaptive Mobility and its employees assume no responsibility for the actions of others which have modified the van. Mr. Lombard admits in his letter that the van only began having the said problem after the warranty expired and after the trailer tow wiring harness was installed.

Adaptive Mobility is the supplier not the converter as stated in Mr. Lombard's letter. We have one location and the plant in reference is the manufacturer of the conversion which since has been sold to the Braun Corporation. Adaptive Mobility performed no modification to said van. Modification to the electrical system was made by Rayco Electronics and it is documented by our service manager that the install of the tow harness by Rayco created the draw. The vehicle was not serviced for this particular problem during the warranty period. In good faith and good faith only, Adaptive Mobility Equipment Inc. is willing to work with a new car dealer of Mr. Lombardi's choice to make arrangements to purchase the trade at the current wholesale market value as determined by Adaptive Mobility Equipment, Inc.

Sincerely,

Dennis Kochanek—Adaptive Mobility, Inc.

Dear Michael,

This letter is an answer to Mr. Dennis Kochanek's letter of Feb. 27, 2008:

First, Adaptive Mobility did the modifications to the van according to Herb Chamber's Ford which leaves them liable for the work performed. Adaptive Mobility and Herb Chamber's service department are complicit in hiding the overdraw on the battery even when the engine was shut off. They knew about the overdraw because they replaced the battery on more than one occasion and had to keep recharging on other performance checks. Jim Cole of Adaptive Mobility said he replaced one battery, Herb Chamber's Ford of Westborough replaced at least one or more batteries, and I had to buy a new battery all before the van had only 8,000 miles on it.

Secondly, Rayco Electronics, Timbuktu, and Lou's Custom Muffler all have stated there is no possible way the wires they installed for trailer lights would cause a draw on the battery. The owner of Lou's is an electrical engineer and he and his wiring guru said that Adaptive Mobility butchered wiring beneath the van. Further, the gentleman who stripped the van down said he would appear in court to testify of the battery overdraw.

Thirdly, as far as the harness is concerned, Adaptive Mobility removed the original one without informing the owner and there was no mention in the contract that they would be allowed to do this. Also, there was a verbal agreement for the van to have a tow bar and wiring installed upon delivery. That was not done, so the salesman told me I would have to do it myself since he stated he lost too much money on his commission in the sale of the van. So this constituted fraud right from day one.

Fourth, Adaptive Mobility endangered my dying spouse with mis-measured installation.

In good faith I have tried working with Ford and Adaptive Mobility, but numerous letters to resolve the problem were never answered over a three-year period.

Since Adaptive Mobility is unwilling to disclose what they will offer for current wholesale value, I have no other choice but to move this case on to a court of law and sue for the incredible mental torture to my dying wife and be reimbursed for an equitable sum since I in good conscience could not sell the van to a handicap person in need of a reliable vehicle.

Respectfully yours,

Ronald L. Lombard Sr.

And now at this present time after talking to my lawyer, who was referred by the Massachusetts Bar Association, it would not be worth my while to pursue this case because the most I could win would be book value on the van, and I might even lose money after paying legal fees. My lawyer, Mr. Stiles, says there is no chance of getting any compensation for mental aggravation, or abuse, especially since so much time has gone by. The reason so much time went by was because both companies hid the fact of the overdraw, which wasn't discovered until after the guarantee was up.

It is my biggest hope that people reading this will be very careful if they need to buy a handicap van and get many opinions before spending so much money.

It is important to note that according to lawyers I have talked to, the number one consumer complaint to the attorney general's office is—you guessed it—the auto industry. Second to that is the housing and building trade.

The following is the letter from Robert Stiles, who was recommended by the Massachusetts Bar Association.

>RE: Potential Litigation
>Dear Ron:
>
>It was a pleasure meeting with you the other day. As I mentioned to you at the close of our meeting on April 16, 2008, I told you that I would follow up with you in writing after I spoke with Michael Lombardi.
>
>I spoke with Michael today. He gave me a brief background regarding his involvement with you and your issue with your Ford van. He told me he tried to negotiate a resolution with Herb Chambers and Adaptive Mobility. He informed me that Adaptive Mobility was willing to work with you to resolve the

issue; however, they agreed only to go so far as to offer to buy back your Ford van at wholesale cost. I understand from you and Michael that this was unacceptable to you.

The facts as I understand them to be are that you purchased a new Ford Windstar van from Herb Chambers Ford on August 6, 2003. You wanted the van to be handicap accessible for your wife so you had Adaptive Mobility do a handicap conversion. I believe you took delivery of the vehicle in November 2003. Sometime in December 2003 you had a tow package installed on the van by rayco. I understand that you had a verbal agreement with Herb Chambers to install the tow package; however Herb Chambers denied the existence of any agreement.

Shortly after taking delivery of the vehicle in November 2003 you began having problems with the vehicle battery. You later learned there was a slow drain on the battery causing it to go dead. You had to replace the battery on a number of ocassions. You brought the vehicle to Herb Chambers for repair; however they informed you that they could not find anything wrong with the van. You had Adaptive Mobility look into the problem and they too said they could not find anything wrong with the vehicle.

You brought the vehicle to Lou's Muffler for a diagnosis. They determined that the cause of the drain on the battery was shoddy work by Adaptive Mobility.

It is my understanding from you that all work to the vehicle occurred during the years of 2005 and 2006. I also understand that you are still experiencing the battery issue today.

I mentioned to you that my primary concern was the amount of time that lapsed from the date you first began having problems with the van. It's been over four years since you first learned of the battery problem. A tort action for negligent services has a three year statute of limitations. Consumer protection claims have a four year statute of limitations. An action on the motor vehicle purchase contract has a four year statute of limitations under the Uniform Commercial code. Based on my review of the law, any worthwhile claim you may have will more than likely be barred by a statute of limitations.

The other issue I mentioned to you was your potential damages and whether or not it was worth you spending money on a lawyer to try and recoup these damages. Obviously you could claim any out of pocket expenses for the purchase of new batteries and any repair bill. If my memory serves me, your repair bills did not amount to much more than $1000. You also had a possible claim for diminution in value of the vehicle as a result of the faulty battery. However, this claim is speculative at best given the fact that you don't know how much a dealer would give you for the van. At the close of our meeting I suggested that you take the van to a Ford dealership and see how much they were willing to give you for the van. Once you had this number, then you could accurately calculate the potential diminution in value. However, even with this information, given the statute of limitation issues, any claim for damages would most likely fail.

Based on the above, I do not believe you have an actionable claim against Herb Chambers or Adaptive Mobility; therefore, I am not willing to accept your case. Please understand that this is only my opinion and that another lawyer may feel differently. Therefore, if you desire to pursue this matter further, I advise you to consult with another attorney immediately. Your other option would be to file a claim in small claims court in Westborough District Court. If you go to court they should be able to assist you with filing a complaint. Be advised that in order to file a claim in small claims court, your damages can not be more than $2000.

Again, it was a pleasure meeting you. I wish you luck in resolving this issue. Please feel free to contact me with any questions.

Sincerely,

Robert K. Stiles, Esq.

So ends a long and sordid journey with Ford Motors, their dealership (Herb Chambers), and Adaptive Mobility. However, the facts don't support Mr. Stiles's claims in his final letter. First, I bought the van from Duddie Ford, who, six months after purchase, sold the dealership to Herb Chambers. Second, I did not have Adaptive Mobility do my conversions. Duddie Ford did. And they violated a verbal contract by not delivering the van with a tow package. They and Adaptive Mobility hid the fact that the vehicle had an overdraw all through the guarantee. Third, the statute of limitations makes this a difficult case because of the van problem wasn't discovered until after the guarantee was up.

Unfinished business can drag the human spirit down with unnecessary negative emotion. I don't judge any one individual, but I felt it was necessary to try and correct a problem, which never should have happened to someone with handicap needs. All the pain that someone causes will reflect back to them before they leave this world. So that is why one should not judge, that's God's job.

# Part Four: A Caregiver's Story Closing Remarks

Events in our life seem to happen on a hit-or-miss basis. After being a caregiver for almost seven years, I now believe it was God's will the way Jackie's and my life unfolded. My wife's illness happened for a reason at the right time in our lives to see her disease to fruition. My being retired early gave Jackie the ability to choose me as her caregiver rather than go into a nursing home. Also, being centrally located in Massachusetts was godsend because of the fine hospice teams that are available in the area. Jackie's primary doctor, Ingrid Fuller, was only minutes away, and this always was a comfort knowing she was so close in case of an emergency. She came to our house on a monthly basis while on hospice and came weekly in the last month, and then daily during the last week of Jackie's life. So I am convinced that my wife had many guardian angels, and it didn't take me long to realize that each and every one of us needs each other, and that we share this earth with all God's creatures. This is what makes America great. It is the universal love, energy, and positive thoughts and ideas that move the majority of Americans to peace, love, and compassion. When the soul of each one of us can see past the ego, greatness spreads throughout the land while negativity and anger can be felt by every thought and idea spread by the ignorant. The multipersonality can see beyond the average thinker. It is love that will sustain us all in our paths to fulfillment, for none of us gets out of this world alive.

Our industrial exploitation gave rise to the well-deserved name Ugly American, while the affluent stifles the middle class and under. Somehow, love will prevail over hate. We will rise above prejudice as the internationalization of the world expands, and freedom and low-cost health care will be made available to all Americans, not just the affluent.

It must be remembered that these matters will get worse if the world doesn't do more to expand population control, for it seems foolish to give donations to feed hungry children without reducing the population explosion worldwide. That is like putting gasoline on a fire, and hoping you have enough water to put it out.

By telling my wife's story, it is my hope as it was Jackie's that our politicians will direct money in the future to stem cell research, which I know will benefit all mankind. Who knows, Congress might even give us the same health care they receive if they can break the stronghold of partisanship and go bipartisan. It's all up to the voters to realize the power they have to move our country forward for the benefit of future generations. For what good is it if you can't make the world a better place to live.

# Acknowledgments

When there is illness in a family, it often brings out the compassion and good energy from friends and neighbors. I would like to thank my next-door neighbors Anne Firmes and D'Arcy McCarthy for their delicious cookies every year that Jackie so loved to sample at Christmastime. Also, thank you, Anne, for being a good friend and visitor to Jackie all those years.

To Evelyn Reiley, thank you for all those wonderful soups and meals that were a blessing and time-saver. Jackie loved and enjoyed your visits and always had renewed energy because of it, and I personally was blessed to have you, Evelyn, and your husband Ed's support during the grievance period. I am especially thankful for your home-cooked meals and making me so welcome during the most difficult time of my life.

To Dot, Ron, and Bob, thank you for being here for Jackie during the most critical months of her illness. Even though she couldn't speak, it meant a lot to just know that you were there for her.

To Marie Davis, bless you for taking care of Jackie with great professionalism and compassion. You are a credit to your profession. Jackie always felt so comfortable and safe in your presence.

It would be difficult to name everybody that played a part in Jackies's care, but I would like to thank a few who spent the most time with her during her last months.

To Dr. Ingrid Fuller, Jackie's primary care doctor: there are people in health care that I think are gifted with divine intelligence to help others and, Ingrid, you were a guardian angel to Jackie. She loved and trusted every decision you made on her behalf and so did I. You came to visit her on a monthly basis and almost on a daily basis in her last week. Jackie and I were blessed and honored to have you guiding us in our most urgent needs.

To Reverend Ted MacNeil and Tomoka Sakai, thank you for participating in Jackie's services. The University of Massachusetts Hospital Hospice is well represented by you both for your compassion and talent.

To Marlene Campbell, thank you for your volunteer work in being a companion and giving Jackie facial massages. We will never forget the beautiful amaryllis plant that you gave Jackie. It kept flowering and made her smile all the time.

To Debbie Mayo, who, for many years, brought Jackie books (from the Shrewsbury library) and movies in her last year. You are a dear friend and a dedicated and qualified employee. Your visits to Jackie always gave her a lift to see an old friend on a steady basis, something that is very difficult when a person can't talk anymore.

To Mary Ellen McClune, Jackie's very talented speech therapist. Your expertise helped Jackie to communicate when she could no longer talk. Identifying dysphagia in its early stages was godsend, and just being a friend was most uplifting for her.

A very heartfelt thank you to all the very qualified nurses and home health aids working with the hospice team from the University of Massachusetts Medical Center that are too many to name but never too tired to give me their time and expertise to keep Jackie pain-free and as comfortable as possible.

To June Bessette, the very talented nurse and massage therapist who gave Jackie great comfort and peace of mind whenever she was at our home. I was honored, as a caregiver, that you would include me for the massage services as well.

To Carol Sazama, whose expertise as a grief counselor helped me sort out the many pitfalls when the going got rough. I am most grateful.

To Anne Ancona and Pam Rososky, for keeping Jackie smiling and laughing most of the time, which was so hard to do when dealing with such a difficult disease. Your expertise in keeping up with each new retrograde was amazing. And most of all, Jackie loved you both as if you were her own sisters. I will forever be grateful and thankful for your compassion and dedication.

To Neil Shailer and Giovanna Witowski, two of the smartest Shrewsbury pharmacy workers I have ever had the honor to do business with, thank you so much for all your support.

To Janet Mullen, for the enormous task of managing one of the most successful hospice teams in central Massachusetts, Jackie and I were blessed to have your expertise and oversight in the final year of Jackie's life.

And finally, to my son Lee and daughter Wendy, thank you for all your time, technical support, and editorial assistance to bring this book to fruition.

Author Ron Lombard Sr.

Get Published, Inc!
Thorofare, NJ 08086
22 January, 2010
BA2010022